Green Revolver

Green Revolver

Worthy Evans

Foreword by David Baker

THE UNIVERSITY OF SOUTH CAROLINA PRESS

*Published in Cooperation with the South Carolina Poetry Initiative,
University of South Carolina*

Published by the University of South Carolina Press
Columbia, South Carolina 29208

www.sc.edu/uscpress

Manufactured in the United States of America

18 17 16 15 14 13 12 11 10 09   10 9 8 7 6 5 4 3 2 1

Library of Congress Cataloging-in-Publication Data
Evans, Worthy, 1971–
  Green revolver / Worthy Evans ; foreword by David Baker.
    p. cm.
  "Published in cooperation with the South Carolina Poetry Initiative,
University of South Carolina."
  ISBN 978-1-57003-932-4 (pbk : alk. paper)
  I. Title.
  PS3605.V3775G74 2010
  811'.6—dc22
                          2010002599

This book was printed on Glatfelter Natures, a recycled paper with 30 percent
postconsumer waste content.

The South Carolina Poetry Book Prize is given annually to the manuscript that
wins the contest organized and sponsored by the South Carolina Poetry Initiative.
The winning title is published by the University of South Carolina Press in coop-
eration with the South Carolina Poetry Initiative.

For Michelle, Matthew, and Elizabeth

Contents

III

Foreword

I am very pleased to present *Green Revolver* to the poetry world. The effects of this book are strong and real, and this collection has stayed with me in a haunting way. So much other poetry, these days, seems too bland and same-sounding, rather like earnest memoirs broken into lines; or, just as common, so many other books seem to be experimental or edgy with no real pay-off and no real reason for their apparently cutting-edge choices. *Green Revolver* impressed me with its confidence, its strangeness, its accruing sense of drama and import. Now these may seem at first counterintuitive compliments, since this book seems to want so badly to be unconfident, casual, even clichéd, and so familiar that we don't notice. But that is its notable achievement: to make poetry from the mundane, the workaday, the familiar (and familial), and the easy-to-overlook. In this book the real becomes hyperreal and, now and then, surreal. Metareal. I take as some of its forebears the poetry of Louis Simpson and Vern Rutsala in his prose poems and perhaps Frank O'Hara. Perhaps this is a South Carolina relative of that urbane, scary, in-your-face New Yorker, Frederick Seidel. Can we make poetry of entirely and decidedly nonpoetic stuff? In the right hands—yes, we can.

These are the right hands, Worthy Evans's. But who is this speaker? He calls himself a "he," and his narrative is specific and seems singular. Yet in one poem he refers to himself as Jeffrey, and in others he is Raoul, Stephen, Rogers (his last name?), Lenny, Mr. Thompson. Call me Ishmael, he may as well say, to embrace the fictive, willful nature of the whole project. At times his wife (or girlfriend) is Dorothy, Monica, Dora, Oma, Charlene, and Mona; and at times he has a daughter named Jeannie, a son named Jeremy or Lonnie, a job (though the job changes), neighbors, hobbies. And all of these things evolve or switch. This poet is a shape-shifting trickster with the voice of the schmuck in the cubicle next door. He might be our savior. He might be the guy in the black robe, holding the scythe. He might be both. So when he speaks in the plural, as he does at times, that choice becomes even more powerful and gathering, even indicting in its collective perspective.

The narrative beneath the surface is, I take it, something about the transitive and generic nature of contemporary life. Nothing in the poems seems more or less important than anything else, and the wonderfully monotone voice—like a newspaper article or a hard-boiled homicide detective's report—presents each thing without judgment, prejudice, or even a sense of difference. Just the facts indeed. The facts are our fate. A job's a job, a boss is a boss, and one's neighbor is as likely to play golf as pull out a machine gun. Is he our barber or a secret agent? "Click, click, click" goes Matthew's toy green revolver in one poem, as though murder and the mundane are names for the same thing. The poems, as they proceed, become more terrifying, if quietly so, for the accruing ennui, the constant routine and rut, the slow building of frustrating and meaninglessness. Little wars break out among the big ones; trauma and anxiety seem like our eventual daily bread; and, even so, something like camaraderie can emerge: the shared plight, if not the shared sympathy, of others with lives similar to ours. There's a frontier wildness to this suburban familiarity. Bison might be delivered by the mailman, and the guy next door might just whip out a revolver.

To match the voice, this poet has developed a kind of ah-shucks prosody, or style. The lines seem casually made, sometimes even a little off-hand, yet they are appropriately shaped for this project. Each poem is a little narrative. Sometimes the story is a commonplace, even tedious account, and sometimes it shocks with the absolute strangeness of its familiarity. In each case the same nonjudgmental voice delivers the news—the bad news—that if we're not careful, we will go mad inside our hypernormal lives.

Green Revolver is an accomplished, distinct, and distinctly eerie collection of poems. I'm happy to offer it to the world as the winner of this year's South Carolina Poetry Initiative competition.

Acknowledgments

I would like to thank the following teachers and friends who provided me laughs, lines, instruction, and inspiration: Paul Allen, Stuart Knee, Clark G. Reynolds, Randy Sparks, George Hopkins, D. Reid Wiseman. Also, my drill sergeants, SFC Gabriel, SSG Snyder, and SSG Dutter.

Thank you, Jack Drost, Angie Gregory, Jason Hendrix, Alicia O'Brien, Sherrie Thompson, Erin McVey, Michelle Neale Mostiller, James Denton, Shannon Rush Aardal, Earl Capps, Lisa Rye, Amanda McGuire, and Caroline Meyer. Thank you to my army pals: Daniel Lonnecker, Scott Connelly, Mark Daly, Marc Greaney, David Pieper, Donovan Lusk, and Andrew Johnson, as well as Clayton Smith, Ronald Moore, and Elmer Pagaragan. Thank you, newspaper veterans Sharon Strauss, Pauline Patrick, Jeff Kidd, Ken Bell, Joe Perry, Gerald Davis, Ron Morris, Robbie Evans, and Dennis Brunson.

Thank you, Kathryn C. W. Scheer and Lloyd Francis Scheer. Thank you, Worthy B. Evans I and Lois Cann Evans. Thank you to my parents, Jack and Mary Evans, and to my sister, May Elizabeth Weatherwax.

"Marooned" appeared as "Buried" in the *James Dickey Newsletter* 25 (Spring 2009).

I

All afternoon you feel the weight of the things you've never done. Don't think about it too much. It starts to sound like a train.

David Shumate, *Trains*

A Funny Thing

My secret fell out from the cuff of my pants
just as I walked up to take the award
for best-dressed, most improved, fullest
all-around role model for the underprivileged,
old people and kids. Everyone stared at my secret,
a pile near the podium set for me to speak.
The clapping died down. There I stood,
all khaki slacks and casual pullover,
looking into thousands of eyes.
I sidled up to the podium, adjusted
the microphone. I wasn't what they said
I was. I never played football. I last made
an honor roll in eighth grade. I learned history
from *Mad* magazines, opera
from Looney Toons, literature from
the Beaver's dad. I can't even find
the degree the college gave me. Busting my knee
in the army kept me out of Korea
and put me on a long road home, where
the SUVs aren't V-8s, aren't even all-wheel drive.
The plantations are neighborhoods.
The bricks amount to a façade. I put everything
on credit and haven't the cash to back it up.
I went on for hours. I must've offended
someone, but no one sitting in the amphitheater

left. I drank all the water the podium
people left for me and was still thirsty.
The crowd walked out, looking intent, as
if they had people of all ages to save. I picked up
my secret from the stage and put it in my back
pocket. Everyone knew what it was now.

The Frontier

I was lost, cold, nervous, wandering
around in the middle of a sprawling city
with no bearings, no money, no idea
where to get a drink of water. Towers
seemed to teeter when I looked up.
I walked past a crew working on one.
I put my face up against a wall with a hole
in it to look in at the construction. Men
and women in neon helmets, bright
vests, jeans and steel-toe boots walked
around. A burly one carrying a bag of
cement over his shoulder stopped,
ripped it open and poured the powder
into a revolving canister. Men tiptoed
around on girders, called up for help,
looked down to direct. A flatbed rolled
onto the job site. Two men and two women
jumped out. All of them going in different
directions after a filling lunch and a moment
at the orange coolers in the shade. They acted
like they knew what they were doing. On their side
I was a face, a portrait of someone not to know.
One of the women even flipped me the bird.
This family built these buildings, and I sit
in them looking out a window at a bird,

a speeding bus. You've got to admire the
stick-to-it-iveness of such endangered species.
I pulled myself from the hole, snapped my fingers.
The man waiting for his bus gave me
his lunch and his wallet.

Marooned

I looked back and it was clear
that I had spent terribly too much time
in the office. I seemed to have
measured the world from the walls
of my cubicle. I watched life go by in
postcards and clipped cartoons,
entire identities clamped onto a cardboard
cutout. Note cards showed me to
the road home. Home being what
work people made the idea of home,
with a few of my leavings in it. A
woman sits beside me with a telephone
to her ear, but she doesn't speak.
She's telling me to relax, take it
easy, find a hobby. I used to build
model ships but that was long ago.
They set sail and left me here to fish
around for the directions to finding
the way out of here.

Comfort

Every summer afternoon I get
a whiff of my own scent. I
smell like sweaty woolen socks,

day-old underwear, wet
cotton and muffled farts.
Other people swear they

can't smell whatever it is
that I'm smelling on me,
but that's OK. I know they

are lying. They are being good
neighbors and are keeping a secret.
Everyone knows they love me,

but let's keep calm. Work must get done.

Croak

Word is out that I'm not such a bad
guy after all, but it's all a lie.
Barb in the office knows in her heart
that I'm a boob. I can't argue when I dropped
a pile of papers she had just organized all over
the floor. I can't dispute that I have
to be shown how to work the Web site
each and every time it's my turn to
update it. Sherrill thinks I'm a
big dreamboat living the life
worthy of a pleasant painting hanging
over a mantle. Randall Fossum,
the landlord, likes that my checks come
on time. The printer who keeps me
employed laughs at my jokes, but he
doesn't know they're not jokes.
The paint is poured on the porch, dripping
down the steps. The car's crashed into
a pole, coolant coloring the road
I rode in on. My arm hangs out
the window, but I'm just waiting for
someone to shake my hand and walk on
into a better life of his own.

Dress for Success

Someone is dressed like me.
Such a heavy burden, to wear
these clothes that someone else wears
without staining or wrinkling the other
person's attire. A baseball hat,
T-shirt and polo pullover, with a
pair of pants that have cargo pockets
stitched on the side: anybody could
wear this. Socks I bought for my
first day of work two years ago,
along with brown hiking low quarters
I got long before the planes hit the buildings
in 2001. Maybe not as many people
could find my footwear. Such a
difficult, terrible weight to bear.

Drip

I was reading the paper in the dining room
this morning, and thinking about all the money
and work we've sank into keeping our home
solid and sound. The coffee tasted rich,
the frosted croissants decadent. I compared the interior
of our house with the ones in the newspaper ads.
I closed my eyes to think where the camera crew
should set up for the upcoming photo shoot
when a drop splashed onto the polished table.
Dorothy was in the shower directly above the
brass chandelier. While she was twisting around
in the steam the drip had gathered its strength
and rolled down the slight bow in the ceiling that
the last contractor said was fixed.
I didn't see this drop develop, but I looked
up at the chandelier to see marks of corrosion.
I reached up and felt the damp sheetrock.
The drip loomed for some time. Dorothy kept
showering. Other drips would come. The table
wobbled. Dust bunnies gathered and stuck
to the damp wooden floor.

Making the Man

Other people wear clothes that
I like, but I try them on and they
never fit. The clothes that fit
make me look like a father, even
if I'm walking into a hotel three
hundred miles from home.
Other people fell out of the hotel
through the years, either because
they wanted to or someone pushed.
I go outside to a sandwich shop
a block away to get the fallen people
out of my head, but after the sandwich
I still have to walk back to the
hotel. I still have to go home wearing
the clothes I have. My shirts balloon.
Shorts too tight in the waist, too loose
in the crotch. Shoes are comfortable,
but trip over wires and kick
against walls. People live better
inside clothes I give up regularly, hoping
I fit somewhere in a home, the way
people fit inside their homes.

Sunset

The man and his wife walked up to the
canyon lip and he said *It's good,*
not great. But the book said to do it
so here we are. The man said he and
the wife got married and later looked
to the west as it stood before Lake
Pontchartrain. *That was better,*
and so was this place in Australia.

The wife until this point had been silent.
She was always the framer and picture
hanger for her husband, she told me as
we were walking back to the gift shop
to look at posters, postcards and
screensavers of what we had just seen.
I believe I'll take this one, she said.

Instructions

If you determine that work procedures
prevent the practice of processing,
treat the request as an inquiry.
Submitting a problem ticket
dismisses this appeal, but must
initiate from inside the QIC.
To determine if the appeal
is a valid appeal, OK the request
and notify that the system is requiring
the reopening. No further argument
to correct the record of your
intent to open a clerical error
is necessary; treat the duplicate as a
hyperlink for the existing
appropriate appeal. Process then,
the open request. Include your
findings in the letter,
then save the file as
a documented inquiry. Repeat.

Camaraderie

The war has never been so close
to me.
    I sat next to a television set turned on
and rolling
    out flickering pictures of three boys
who knew
    each other their entire lives. They dizzied
themselves
    in beer and danced with women all
around them.

    When no war had called me, I saddled up and
ruckmarched
    all over a fort, past motorpools, POVs,
dustbowls, dialogues
    between sergeants and trainees. I ate
food from
    pockets. I got fat and busted
my knee
    and then nobody wanted me.

Lost on a highway
    home, I forgot how to personally be.
I watched TV.

He heard a boom, saw a dust cloud
reduced to results
    run across the screen. The war has never
been so close
    to me.

Erno and Me

Erno sat paralyzed
on the thick-painted
bench outside the station.
I knew him as athletic,
jumping rope, throwing
around a medicine ball.
But that was thirty years
ago, action trapped in photographs
his buddies took aboard his ship.
Erno sits on the bench
Every day and watches
the trains roll by. *I saw*
my grandson head out
of here when all he had
were eyes that looked
back at me from the
bottom of the window,
he said. Since then the grandson
grew large and burly, albeit far
away from this little hamlet
where Erno talked to me.
He's not going to return,
He said. *He could be on every train*
that rolls by, but he'll never
come back. I looked at myself

in the washroom mirror
of the tiny depot. I had to be sure.
I felt weak and delirious,
having seen Erno, alive,
on a marvelous golden day.

Nature

A residence at Brook Farm does not involve either a community of money, of opinions, or of sympathy. The motives which bring individuals there, may be as various as their numbers.
Charles Lane, writing for the Dial, *January 1844*

I would've always listened to her
but I sputtered around drunk,
driving into the idea that above all

man should be free. I walked for a
while, fell in love with the sound of my
cadence, laughing when flattened arches

fell, at least I had the feet God blessed me
with for a while. I would've then
always listened to her but I dawdled

around doing odd jobs to pay the bills
I always had to foot. There came a
wedding, there came the children, but

it was always her way of reminding me
that they could have my husk and
what grew inside it for a while, but

then will come a time I will fall
back into her forever arms and she
will hold me, sweet Lord, finally.

Heroes in Waiting

I felt a sickness in the back of my
throat when I woke up. I popped
a pill and went into the shower. By
the time I got to work the sickness
reached my stomach, but I had
no couch on which to fall. We
had to see about changes in
a computer application that
weren't in the program yesterday.
None of us knew exactly what to
do. The poster said we were
heroes in waiting and needed a pat
on the back. Teamwork classes
included catching each other as we're
falling off of porches. All of us, though,
gathered around a big box and put
our hands in. What we felt, we
had to fix. But first we had to
identify what it was we held.
I became dizzy, delirious, fumbling
around over necks or nuggets
of unknown substance. Hero worship
put on hold. I fell to the floor with
all of these arms touching me,
finding me out.

Pre-Op

Dan Jones is coming to meet with us.
All of us, Monday at 2:30 P.M. Dan
Jones will meet with all of us two
days from now. It is all we were
told. Neil Diggs walked up and gave us
the tip, but he didn't say why Dan
Jones was going to meet with us,
or who Dan Jones is and what
kinds of business Dan Jones was
after. Dan Jones could be a barber, and
for all I know that's what he is. I looked
down to see what Dan Jones did to me,
the hair on the floor, a drop of blood
smeared onto my pant leg when the clipping
became fierce. I heard opera music and
saw a delicate white hand cross over
cold steel instruments resting on the soft linen.
Tulips grew in the garden outside
the window where Dan Jones, the faculty
and I were meeting to discuss budget cuts.
All of us topping our shaggy manes until Dan Jones
rides by on his penny-farthing to give us a clip.

At Any Moment

For every ten workers who show up each morning to work in this particular building, there's one worker missing every so often. How does a worker know he is the missing one? Anyway, every week all employees are required to log in to a Web site and answer one question having to do with the security of our building, our offices, our files, our livelihood in relation to the government contract that is kept somewhere, but no one knows where except for Mr. Foxworth. The question originated from a hodgepodge of ideas that centered around keeping on our toes, watching out for offending persons, making sure our secrets never become published. *What do you do at the end of each day with regard to our company's sensitive information?* I made that one up. *Destroy it* was the answer I was looking for. I make them easy, so everyone can feel knowledgeable in the keeping of secrets. Each time they answer correctly, they rejoin the brotherhood. We want to ensure our employees are capable of performing the tasks that they are given, but we don't want them to feel stupid about their job, looking over their shoulder. That was the point of starting up these quizzes eight months ago. Since then, however, I've noticed something different about the office. Joe Laruda from accounting says that when you get an answer incorrect, the liquidation crew comes to get you. How preposterous, I thought. What poppycock. *How do you know, then, not to blow a whistle, or make a scene, or notify authorities outside of our employment? That's the thing that's creepiest,* Joel said. *The liquidators are crack. You don't*

even see them coming. They hear you before you sense their presence. And
they have duplicitous ways of deleting your knowledge of them or of your
coworkers and employees. They are the real hands of this company, unless
you consider Mr. Foxworth himself. Henry Foxworth is an uncom-
plicated man. He wears wire-rimmed spectacles and dresses in
loafers, khaki pants and button-down shirts of various colors.
He walks around the building often, quick with a smile and a pat
on the back. I had a hard time thinking that Mr. Foxworth could
be the very entity tapping us for termination. Just last week he
had given a lily to, to, someone. And once I saw him help . . .
someone else . . . pick up a pile of paper spilled in the hall.
Henry Foxworth got us all to give to the United Way. He sent
e-mails to tell us what to contribute to any charity he deemed
fit. There was no kinder person in this building.

I explained to him that I clicked the wrong answer by mistake.
I looked straight into his cool face, his loving eyes. He was
    an angel.
I felt his touch on my back, then he shuffled away.

II

SUSANNE: David! David! Those feelings!
DAVID: Into the woods!

Equinox (1970)

Baked into the Cake

The bride was kissed. The cake
was eaten. Lula had completed
her customary belly dance and
there arose such an emotional
reception that tears came to my
eyes in delight. As these things do,
the good feeling died down and I
caught on to the one-way conversation
about doorknobs. Phillip the
bartender, he listened in too, after
serving me up a gin and tonic.
Marshall Weinstein, of the Kensington
Weinsteins, had clinked a glass and
begun the downhill slide into doorknobs.
Sometimes we encounter crystal
doorknobs that you need only push
to open the door, which had long since
swelled beyond the jamb. I began
to feel ill. *Brass ones gleam brightly,*
but oh, the polishing that we must
do. Marshall was up front, beside
Regina Whittingham, nee Winkleman,
and I was near the door at this
reception in the basement of a redone
barn. There were no doorknobs here.

The iron doorknobs with patterns
stamped upon them turn black over
time, get lost in sock drawers, where
little children mistake them for turtles.
He laughed at this, maybe remembering
some unprompted discovery after his dad
had gone to work. I remember missing
Lula's belly dancing, so in a twist in my chair,
I looked out the unlatched door at a mother
hen waddling around with her chicks.
My son isn't going to like her.

Occurrences Around the Bridge

He was now in full possession of his physical senses. They were,
indeed, preternaturally keen and alert. Something in the awful
disturbance of his organic system had so exalted and refined them
that they made record of things never before perceived.
                        Bierce, "An Occurrence At Owl Creek Bridge"

Around 9 A.M. I pulled into the Jiffy Mart
to get the breakfast of breakfasts, a Polish
sausage and a large coffee. I plinked
the sausage from the hot roller, wedged
it into a bun and folded it up into a box
made of styrofoam. I poured coffee,
put a lid on it, then walked up to the cashier.
Vinny looked up at me, held a gaze while
blindly ringing up my goods. $2.39. Did Vinny
tap something under the counter? I paid cash,
left a penny, got back in the truck. *Good morning!*
I said to the tanker driver. He made time
to look up and nod. I turned onto Broad
Street. A woman in a PT Cruiser stared at,
then winked, at me. I turned on the radio
and heard the story about the helicopter.
The woman at the library said she was
thrilled with the donation. I turned onto
Needham Street and tossed the hot dog box

on the floor. At twenty after nine I made
a phone call to my lawyer. *Jeffrey, no matter
where you are or what you're doing, stop it
and come to me. We can work this out,* he said.
Go fuck yourself, I said. I saw the gray car,
but didn't stop. The Hyundai, Saturn, whatever
model it was, hung behind. More on the radio
about the helicopter. The traffic was backed up
because of the accident. Maybe it was too late,
just as I had thought. Quarter to ten and the sky
blasted sunlight white. I put on sunglasses
I found at the Goodwill. I pulled it all together
and tried the expressway, but it was backed up further.
The cameras over the lanes clicked. Three killed
and the pilot taken to the hospital, another radio
bulletin announced from another helicopter. The homeless
vet in the middle of the road took donations.
Extended deployment keeps thousands away
from home another three months. The post officer
down below the expressway is running the flag
up the pole. A kid in the back window of a Volvo
looked at me and winked. Half past eleven I inch
off the crosstown as some Joes on a construction
crew salute me. A car alarm sounds. Nearing noon
I've made it through the loops turns and stops.
I pull into another Jiffy Mart around noon for the lunch
of lunches. I have to use the bathroom. The reverend
tells me, *May God have mercy on your soul.*

Fall In

Discipline is the cornerstone on which the Army is built. To be
successful in the Army you must develop your discipline far above
that required in civilian life.
   IET (Initial Entry Training) Soldier's Handbook, *1994*

Not long after I strapped on my helmet and hefted all my issue
up into the basket, there came a holler that it was time for us
to run. I already wore the running shirt, but my shorts were
stashed somewhere into my barracks bag around my bunk.
The building was all wood. The bunks and lockers made the
place a labyrinth of lost places. Wire baskets full of blankets
and unstowed clothing littered the room. I heard the cries
to assemble, to it now, come as you are, bring what you have
the run is on and we cannot deviate from the training schedule.
And so, wearing boots and long pants and a dirty shirt, I ran
out to see a bunch of well-fed men who looked like
paper cutouts of me in my better days, when I had muscles
and no slump. Single file, we began marching, then
hopped into a light jog, and then sprinted to a full-out run.
I thought the run was to make us leaner and more ready
when the time came, but I looked behind us. A fresh
    platoon was
moving in. They had gotten into town yesterday on

their schedule, and they had come looking like one another, looking for us, ready for Victory. Always an objective in mind. No garrison duty for them. Today they were thrilled to see us.

Buffaloed

Six bison calves that escaped from a local farm at 2 A.M. Thursday, crossed U.S. 278 and spent the day roaming greater Bluffton, were shot to death after attempts to corral and sedate them failed. . . .

Authorities tried tranquilizing the animals before the family and law enforcement decided to euthanize them. . . .

Hilton Head Island Packet, *May 23, 2008*

I

It wasn't until noon when the mailman
parked the truck and walked up to my
door to deliver the buffalo. *Bison,*
Mr. Thompson. There are differences,
he said. *Did any letters come explaining*
his care and feeding? I said. *She should*
do well with a little water and a lot
of prairie grass, he said. He gave me
the rope to the animal. She reared
back and skipped when the mailman slammed
down the mail truck's tailgate. *How do you*
know so much about buff, uh, Bison, I shouted.
He hopped up on the driver's side
of the truck. *He has been a part of my*
life for a dozen years, Mr. Thompson.
Without her I wouldn't be the mailman I am.

33

She looked at me, a lump of skull and hair
between her black eyes. Some civilizations
consider her delicious. And warm. Binding
a community the way her sinew would pull
together her hide over a case of well-crafted poles.
She was easily worth more than a nickel. She
was a part of the city. Ironically unsurprising,
like a lump on the back of your head you expected
to come from a pistol whip in the dark.
My love, I said.

II

Oma was in the kitchen cleaning up
after breakfast when Lonnie tore in
from his cartoons in the living room.
There's a big animal in our yard!
Oma knew in an instant the Buffalo had
come. *A buffalo, dear. It is meant for
us. Can I ride it,* Lonnie asked.
This buffalo is not the riding kind,
Oma said as she studied it from the
kitchen window. The buffalo stood
as if it were the one on the nickel
Dad found and gave to Lonnie
for his collection. The buffalo in
the yard talked, in its own way,
about his many uses. Bones for
needles and weapon tips, sinew
for string and thread, muscle for
nourishment, organs for bags and
toaster oven cozies, hide for picnic
awnings, horns for cups, hair for sweaters.
When he finished talking, he hunched
down on all fours and stared into a daisy.
I need you to help me understand all of this,

the buffalo whispered into Oma's ear. He pointed
a hoof out to the traffic on Highway 170.
Oma took Lonnie by the shoulder blades
and pushed him back into the house.
She knew enough to get into the house
and get the rifle.

III

The hooves set off a silent alarm.
Men set out with searchlights
to find the trail that had to be
stamped out of a dense thicket
of pines, myrtles and brambles—
every variety. By dawn the calls
came in. Javier from the golf course
smelled the odor and took pictures
as they grazed the thirteenth fairway.
Charly Powter phoned in one tearing up
her freshly laid sod. We dispatched
searchers on horseback when she was not
convinced of her incredible gift. She
still believes in grocery stores and shoe
outlets on the highways. Charlene's cans
in the pantry, her elephant car in the
yard, enough for us to know the
buffalo held no honor in this home.
The herd ran faster than our horses
could pursue. They feared our
speeding Navigators and Explorers.
For this fear and flight we took up
our rifles and we shot them down.

Green Revolver

Four weeks ago Matthew moved
some bones from the back yard
to the front yard. Three weeks ago he
helped his mom around the house,
picking up laundry, throwing loose paper
away. She gave him two dollars.
Two weeks ago I took him
to a dollar store. Matthew walked back
to the wall of dime toys and found
a green revolver, little gray blackjack
and gold handcuffs, shrink-wrapped against
an upbeat cardboard law-enforcement sign.
One week ago he climbed into the truck
with his revolver that he constantly
clicked. He left it there when I pushed him
out for school, and it sits here right now,
on the seat. Every person talking about work
on the walking trail, every mocking bird,
every passing car, click, click, click.

On the Weekend

I was leaning toward Jeannie
to tuck her in when she sprung
up and gave me a left cross.
The surprise of it, more than the meat
of her balled fist, threw me back over
the baby carriage, where I met the
shelf full of books that ended
with Happily Ever After. I thought
of rainbows and laser beams, mushroom
cakes and cookie salad she made for me
in her kitchen the day before. Liking it
was never enough. All of it was a lie. She was
in waiting, poised to punch me out and hurl me
out of her musical in the works. I didn't look
to see if she was still in bed or following
up with a bronco-busting daddy ride down
the steps. So I crawled into Jeremy's room
to see if our boy was awake. I found him
standing over me, holding two beakers
of different-colored fluid. *Which is*
the fruit juice and which is the soy sauce,
right? I asked. He poured both beakers on me.
When I awoke my face was buried
under several layers of bandages.
I watched plus signs and kaleidoscopic

snowflakes develop from the back of my
eyelids until I felt a presence, heard a voice
from the foot of the bed. *Lenny honey,*
this is Dora, your wife, it said.
We've all recovered from our missteps.
I want you to know we're all waiting for
you to come home. I began to cry as
the quiet came back to the room, but I was
a man with a puffy head and no face.
A few minutes later I heard the flipping
of a magazine, and footsteps.

Bilderbergers

There came a knock at the door
right about the time I wondered
if anyone knocks on a door anymore.
I opened it and found Ethan
standing but rocking back and forth.
We need to talk, Raoul, he said.
This is not the time, Ethan, I said. *Now
is never the time. You have your orders.
Go ahead and shoot me.* Ethan said *it's
not that, Raoul, I'm not the one who
pulled that string. I was the one with
the shortest string. We're both in trouble
and we've got to get out of here.* I had
just put a roast in the oven when he
said this, so naturally, I was flummoxed.
There was so much to leave behind.
How long do we have? I asked. *Not long,
that's for sure. I just left the convention
with Arthur and the marchers
were walking to the cars,* Ethan said. *Where's
Arthur,* I wondered aloud. *He drew
the short string. I pushed him into the
boxwood when we came around the corner.
I noticed his disorientation, but it can't be
long before he comes to his feet and*

sets it in motion, Ethan said.
I don't know about Arthur. I never
appreciated his lack of temerity, I said.
Well, Raoul, I suppose you should begin
to appreciate it, Ethan said.
He looked out the screen door, paused
for a moment, then jerked his head to
me. *I see his hair now. A gangly mop,* I said.
He's slow enough, but he's coming, shotgun
unloaded but shells bulging from his coat,
Ethan said. *Only time will tell,* I laughed.
Slow and steady wins the race.

Outer Marsupials

I must be peculiar for a secret agent.
I sign my name to just about every document
that came under my hands. Receipts, checks,
handbills, hotel registers, all of them I mark,
Mr. Lawrence Delmore. People know me as Larry.
I speak openly of civic engagements and have never
dodged a camera or a reporter. I make dutiful
notes and send them to reporters so they can
determine my whereabouts and extrapolate my
doings. I make it obvious that I am not
a secret agent. Every newspaper reports
my coming and going. I do have my
enemies, but they know me only as Walter Ng,
38, of Nantucket. Targets for assassination know
about the marks I make on them, but they
invited me to their islands anyway,
and I kill them.

The Lost Weekend

Charlene picked it out. Three hundred
miles from Washington, a two-room
cabin on a hillside covered with ash
and poplar trees. The forest air smelled
green and fresh. I went out for a walk while
Charlene stayed around the cabin looking
for a place to put all of our baggage. I heard
movement in the woods as night began
to fall—a ruffling of leaves, a snapping
of branches. No humanity was around
me, but the sounds were loud enough
to have been a platoon. The snapping
and rustling grew louder as I hiked back
up the hillside. I wished I had brought my
revolver, but I didn't think a lost weekend
in the woods meant that I be armed and
awaiting danger. There was a gunshot, then
another and another. Pop-zing, the rustle
and snap grew louder. I heard otherworldly
growls and grunts. I picked up my stick,
brought it close to my body, put my weight
on my back leg and brought the stick down
—charge bayonets—the way the army taught
me. More breathing and wheezing, the rustle
became legs and feet dragging through the

forest floor. I made sure to show conviction
in my eyes. They would never take me alive.
My palms sweated, my stomach churned. My
three-hundred-pound body felt light.
I felt a thud on my shoulder. Just as quickly as
the warrior tumbled into me, he stood up
and ran down the hill. Two other men
breezed past me. They were both red-eyed,
terrified, like they had seen the devil.
I gathered myself and scaled the hill, searching
for Charlene. The cabin stood among arms,
legs and heads detached from bodies.
My heart sank. I gathered myself
and opened the cabin door. Charlene sat
in a rope chair smoking a cigarette, naked
and bloodstained. *What kept you, honey?*

Go to War

I walked into the motorpool office
whistling, flipping an apple I swiped
from the chow hall up and around.
The move was on. Two mechanics
had grabbed hold of an eight-foot-tall
iron shelf, one of several we used to
divide the large room into three offices.
All the doors to the office were open,
even the one I walked into and shut
reflexively. Two other mechanics had
begun painting the gray cinderblock
wall a darker shade of gray. Captain
Tilby, who ran the motorpool from his
loft office, peered out of his doorway.
Move those shelves back about three
feet, he said between the hammering.
I looked for the soldiers I worked with.
All were gone. Captain Tilby saw me
and came down from the steps. *It's*
about time you've showed up. We need
you to move your truck, he said. *Where to?*
Where's my key? Where is everyone I know?
I asked. *I know you'd like to know, but we*
haven't got any time for that, Tilby said.
Well, I need the key to the truck if I have to move

it like you want me to, sir, I said. *That's*
an outstanding point, Rogers. I'll see to it
that you get it in my last will and testament.
And by God, you'll get a medal for this, you'll
see. His mind seemed clouded with dozens
of logistical operations, getting the tracks
and blades dispatched, moving the mechanics
into the motorpool bays, requisitioning extra
engines, drives, tires, canvases and gasoline.
He began formulating without finishing
his sentences, but somewhere in between I
understand that he wanted me below, to wait
out the movement, face the changes, lone soldier
that I was in a bay full of replacements. I looked
at them. Rubber faces and shaved heads. Straight
out of basic and into the office. *This is going*
to be a new century of death among all of us,
I toasted, having pulled out my canteen from one
of the wall lockers. Pau and Tamalden looked
down from their ladders and winked.

Cougar Dan

He came, we were told, riding in from
the badlands, twirling pistols on his fingers,
riding sideways on a horse that was faster
than lightning. Cougar Dan careened through
the streets, steadying his guns
and leveling them on anything his fingers
desired to see ushered to kingdom come.
He stormed into the Church of the Blessed
Redeemer before heading to raise Cain
on a cattle drive. There he was, pinwheels
and sparklers, heehaws and hoo-has,
staccato shots at the tabernacle.
Then Father Mike closed the doors
and locked Cougar Dan in with all of us.
He thumped and jingled his spurs up and
down the aisles, shot out the windows,
threw out his knives from the secret sheaths
in his sleeves. All the candles snuffed, he fell
to his knees and cried. Our ears began to bleed.
He'd come in here to look for pleasure seekers
and trapped like a calf, he lunged at us and beat
himself against us. We pushed him into a corner
where he beat his shoulders furiously until

he fell asleep. About that time we'd
all had our fill of Cougar Dan. We played
with his cat and turned it loose
on the town.

Camera Crew

We wanted a little of everything.
Film of hands holding lit cigarette
stubs, people in the parks,
at the outdoor café, hands of bodies
leaning against the building, bodies stooped
over messy gin and tonics at the bars
down in the Basin District. When
we had all of the smoking hands,
open mouths and slumping bodies
we could stand, we singled out
walking waistlines. We found people
standing in line and sitting in the shade
by the riverside in the mid-afternoon.
We shot a pod of people sitting
inside an office bay, staring into
flickering monitors. Then we packed it up.
We stowed the gear in the van and found
a tavern, ate sandwiches, sat around,
smoked, drank, ate more before heading
back to the office in the morning.
Past midnight I stumbled into the motel room
and flipped on the TV. Housing market down
20 percent. Smoking banned in public places.

Heart attacks and strokes more likely among us.
Our people are on. Lined up, wondering
what to do, lighting up and pacing.
We're walking awkwardly to the beach
to think about *something*.

Finely Educated

Monica and I had finally got
around to sitting in a restaurant
and eating dinner. Marvin gave
us menus and sat us at the table
closest to the fountain. Artie
the violin player was on the other side
of the open-stone fireplace,
and through the crackling flame
I could see him from his fingers up and down
the fingerboard. He was a true
master, working the bow across
the body of his gleaming mistress.
He made her sing melancholy
notes as Joe and Mitzi from
the car wash incident scooped into
their sorbet. Monica unfolded
her napkin and placed it over her
lap, but I didn't see what she held
in her hand until she snapped
her fingers in my face to get me
out of the fire. *Stephen, hello.*
She sounded like my third-grade
teacher. Miss Bentner commanded
a classroom, but she always
liked to hear me stumble across

"Shortnin' Bread" on the violin,
when I could finally play it.
Monica looked particularly stern,
her hair up in a messy
pile. The longer Artie played
on the violin, the more envious I became.
I may have sat across from Monica,
but he was getting the A.

Once upon a Time

*The future don't matter to us. Nothing matters now——not the
land, not the money, not the woman. I came here to see you. Cause
I know that now, you'll tell me what you're after.*

Frank, from the movie Once upon a Time in the West

Right when Henry Fonda looked at the camera
with both guns drawn, Cecilia called and asked
me to meet her downtown. *It's Dave,* she said
when I walked into the diner. *He's dying. I don't
know what to do. I'm so sorry, Cici,* I said.
I never know what to say when a husband like Dave
suddenly is dying in a midnight diner. *He's got
some time yet, but they say it's no use. He's going
to go soon.* Cecilia was taking this pretty hard,
although before the news of his dying she had
divorced him seven years ago. *He can't do this,*
she said. *He can't do this. This was done and now
he's come back. It's like he never left.* She wept. I tried
to be of some comfort, but all I could do is fiddle with
an empty cream pitcher while she went on. In the lull
I spied on the cook doing time in front of the burners.
He worked efficiently, moving a loaded omelet pan
into the oven while smashing around hash browns
and flipping through a half-dozen flapjacks on
the griddle. *He never really left, you know,* I said.

Just when you think he's gone, he comes back again
and again. Just then Dave walked in. *Rumors of my death,*
he began but tailed off. He was obviously lit. He jiggled
two quarters into the Wurlitzer by the door. "Love Me Do"
opened up and he mimed a mean harmonica opener.
I know you, I said. *You've come from my past*
to avenge the death of your brother. That's when I knew
that I was the dead man, no matter how any
script doctors in this story would write it.

Making Do

We few, we happy few . . .
    Shakespeare, Henry V

There were only a few of us left,
And the outlook was not bright.
We had them on the run, but they
outfoxed us. They turned around,
headed us off at the pass, then
bushwhacked us just when we were
on a roll. We lost our rank and
file, tumbled down the hill like marbles
hurled from the sky. When they rained
down grapeshot, gunnysacks
could not collect the fibers of our
being. Cut down in the valley, we
pulled ourselves out from our pant legs.
We picked up the remnants of our rifles
but whispered inside of us this was enough.
Our leader, spilling the silt from
his brogans, wrapped us all around
him and from within these vines and
thicket he placed his hands on our
failing heart. *We were beaten in every*
way we could possibly imagine. We
have among us only a few rounds

and a handful of means to an end. We
thought this was a great idea and now
we're picking out the burrs in our butts.
But today is a feast day. Today a person
from our country thought of a great
device to keep us rolling, to enliven
our conversation to grant us peace
and to secure our liberty. Somebody else
decided to celebrate that day with a feast
of many meats and vegetables, bread
high in fiber and all of it without any
trans-fat. He died. But other people
lived to celebrate this feast, and create
other feasts on the following days.
With those feasts came sales and
zero-percent financing. We invested
in high-yield bonds and later
dabbled in housing securities. We refused
to regulate the Internet and celebrated
paranoia, one nation under surveillance,
from then until now, when
obscurity surely rests at our feet.
Hushed, we looked up at the
forces beginning to pin us down and
knew there was only one thing to do.

III

They lay there,
the two, in bondage, in disgrace. And some one,
not the least humorous of the gods in Heaven,
prayed that some day he might be overtaken
by such disgrace himself. And there was laughter
for a long time in Heaven, as the story
was told again and again.

Ovid, "The Story of Mars
and Venus," from *Metamorphoses,*
translated by Rolfe Humphries

The Lesson

Four hundred trainees bound for war
filled sections H through K in the ballpark,
ready to take in a game.

Time to pitch security notions
and pulling guard to watch college
boys in summer leagues

take a break and beat each other with
wooden bats and tricks rubbed up in the dirt.
The trainees holler the Soldier's Creed

at attention, and got to the pitcher in
the fifth. His slider down and in went too far,
too hot to handle for his catcher, who

pounced a mitt on the ball just as the
runner at second jumped for third. Catcher rifled
too hard around the right-handed batter

and the bullet sailed away from the third
baseman and into left. Leftfielder threw
to catcher but by then our runner rounded

the bag and set his sights on home. When
the ball bounced back in, the run was on
the board. Some pats on the back,

fist bumping, bucking up. It's only one run,
shake it off babe, shake it off. Four hundred
soldiers seated in H through K wrap up

their chant. Ball in hand, focus back on
the batter, pitcher looks in, lesson learned.

The Madman's Divining Time

After the rain, we walked out onto
the patio. The air was still wet
and the bark of the fat pine tree
was streaked with hits and misses. I've never
seen our backyard so green and liquid.
Mona checked her plants to see
if the passing shower gave them anything
at all. She worked her thumbs into the pots
of petunias, pansies, marigolds
whatever they were, a wild palate of color
mixed and matched by a madman.
He has a plan for us, Mona said.
With each shower he carves us up
into little pieces and shows us colors we
never knew we were. I looked down
at the thin puddle on the porch. In the twilight
I was a muddle of ruddy bumps
and sandy dribbles of gray hair.
Mona, of course, showed herself in blues and
oranges, ochre, velvety red, peach,
jasmine and touches of deep purple
where the setting sun steals the other colors

away. Maybe, if I worked the dirt up
under my fingernails, there
would be hope for me. Mona had
already left the deck and soared off into the
leftover sunshine to dance with that fiend.

In Line

The microphone is just a badge.
Nobody says anything around golf
courses anymore. The winner comes
off the eighteenth green and tips his hat,
which is the signal to his manager
to start handing out copies of
what the champ said about his
day. Reporters don't complain.
Oh, quite the contrary. The canned
copy does make for a quicker day.
One time though, one golfer thought
too much of himself. He talked all
the time, through his rounds, getting
ready to tee off. A heavy drinker,
a ball slammer, a grip-it-and-rip-it
fun guy. Winning a tournament gave
him reason to win another and another,
filing stories may as well have been
copying press releases word-for-word.
When he hit short on the final hole
at Augusta National, he blew his chance
for his second straight Masters win.
He was all humble, glad-handing the next
young heavy-hitting phenomenon.

He showed up at a fundraiser in a wheelchair
two days later. He never golfed again.
The press guys found him outside the bar
where he celebrated his victory and beat him
senseless with his own clubs.
Goes to show you, they all said.

Jury Room

The guy I thought was a lawyer was
unemployed. The concert
promoter sits at a folding table
and makes his case for
getting the museum *to extend its*
Arms toward us. The soldier drinks
a diet soda and eats peanuts.
Schoolteachers see Hillary Duff
in a photo spread. The skinny woman
in the brown dress sits down
with a *Ladies' Home Journal.*
She extended the invitation.
We are a very low-maintenance
organization. We want performers
who are good and low-maintenance,
the promoter continues. A cross-dressing man
fills out a check in a book. Resolved, the ladies
discriminated in that printing office years
ago. The judge may ask of us some embarrassing
things. The promoter's cell phone goes
off. He'd checked the list, he's able
to fit us in. Prospective jurors return. They begin

folktales of a judge telling each to speak
his name. The head of newspaper circulation
looks at the wall, gives directions in her absence.
The rest of us are given a telephone number.
We are told to call it tonight.

From Assembly

It begins in prison with the obligatory
mention of barbeque. There arise
highways and hounds beside the confluence
of rivers. Deserted people talk about the
lottery and life on the rebound. Thousands
come out to see the Gamecocks get punched
in the stomach with a Bulldogs touchdown
on a handoff on fourth and two. A sportswriter
fired from an apparel magazine gets off
the couch. The continuance of Saluda
and Congaree goes rocky before their divorce.
A wreck in the water continually happening
as vehicles speed by until they pass Elmwood
Cemetery. These parts are all replaceable,
but the problem is they are already committed
to the people next door. Gates open to
Olympia, beyond the bayonet of the Great War
rifleman. The weakened mayor limits
himself to the territory the town
council calls to his attention. I walked
into a concrete box across from the IHOP
to interview for an outdoors magazine.
Cannons trained toward the Capital City
landed some shells before the surrender.
The buildings burned thereafter. I liken the

damage to the sound a freight train makes
hitting the water from the flood plain
that washed the cargo away. The governor
covered in topcoat overlooks
the continual damage. *We will never
surrender,* he finds. His motto re-carved
into the granite gets scraped onto the
walk again. We float economic resurgence
onto the equal opportunity
employers. It never hurts to ask.

Passing Through

There was a threat, an action, a declaration
of war. I slept through physics and woke
up in snow. I looked at my white canvas
uniform, painted helmet, rifle and whitewashed
equipment when I got up. Others were dressed
the same way, so I did what they did. We had
fully surrounded this brick bungalow, when Colonel
Flor told us to dig into the snow. *We haven't
much time. The future of our families,
our country, our place in the world, depends
upon what we do here,* he said. *We must
always refuse to negotiate, we must always
strive for excellence.* Everyone else hollered
Essay ons except for me, because I was still
waking up. All of us, though, seemed to see
the upper hand wending its way into our lives.
We broke our backs carving our trenches.
We sank our bodies into the frozen clay.
Our V-shaped trenches, Captain Parrott told
us, gave us the best chance of survival. *I'll
believe that shit when I see us get out
of them,* Carroll said after pounding in his
aiming stakes. Our fire patterns interlocked
within the contested field. If we kept from
shooting each other, our fire would cover

the house. I looked at the portal glowing
from out of the left window. *Thar she blows!*
Munger said. *I guess it's never too late
to plan your final expenses,* I tacked on,
finally getting into the thick of it. We did
all we could, but then came the reckoning.
Oddly shaped faces beamed out of the
windows. The bulbs from the swinging chandelier
were the first to go. The bed, dresser and kitchen
table slid in and splintered into nil. Books fluttered
like birds, then poofed into dust. The house shook
off its foundation and zipped into naught.
I hunkered down and curled up in my hole.
The dirt wasn't going anywhere. I felt
my wet breath rise up my rifle and disperse. Where
there are things that pull, there must be things
that push. Not here for very long, and I was going
to get pulled and pushed into somewhere else.
I had smoked my cigarettes, kissed my babies
goodbye, looked to welcoming my new home.

Strange Days

My name is Lucius McGreevy
and I am seven feet tall. I love
to eat small animals after I shoot
them with my high-powered rifle
and did I tell you I went on a blind
date yesterday? The tape went on,
the recording blotted out in places
with paper-wadding racket
and other breathy voices. A jingling
that sounded a lot like keys on a ring.
I didn't know what to think.
Mr. President, this recording may parallel
your recent speech at the governor's
birthday party, General Akmanzadar
said. *There were certain signatures*
and references that we verified before
giving you this for your listening
pleasure. Lucius McGreevy was
a troublesome sort. Always with the
bombings, always telling us we eat
too much and watch too much TV.
The news channel flipped on a transcript
of the tape that I had been listening to.
I stopped listening and read. The reunion
tour had been cancelled with the birth

of twins. All systems were go on
the shuttle launch. The farm bill went
down to defeat. More and more soldiers
from the front were complaining of
multi-rhythmic incantations from inside
their Kevlar-coated heads. *These are
strange days indeed for the Artimor
administration,* I laughed. My daughters
had learned to drive, my son was home
from college. I walked outside my office
to look for another recording
from our little friend.

Stand To

I was half buried deep in the forest
when the bombs started to drop.
Not that I was scared or nervous.
The bombs started to drop far away
from me, in a city by the coast, where
all the luxurious targets go to die.
At least they would be tan, well-fed.
I was half buried, deep in the forest
within a thicket no tank would undertake,
and I had a helmet on my head. I was out on
the perimeter, weapon facing the enemy
whom I knew at any time could lunge over
the wires and stick their bayonets into my
thicket like it were harvest time. No movement
this morning. We have been waiting for hours
to hear something we weren't supposed
to ever hear, should the right people
have been paying attention atop their towers
in the city by the coast. They will get theirs
when the bombs start to drop? No. Those people
are well-trained, will walk toward the fallout shelters
sixty feet below the surface. They'll be all right.
Children will be playing in the parks tomorrow,
everyone fed and watered, good cattle. This is
a typical day in the service of my country.

Last Seconds

We could all swim in the lush
blue carpet, but we felt the rush
of patriotism and stood up
when the press secretary
walked in and stood at the
podium. *The president will*
not be making an appearance but
feels like the best tack to be
taking is one of helpful de-
aggression, Secretary McMiniver
began. *He states the proper*
analogy should be taken from
his favorite sports. There's a
field goal to be kicked in the stadium
designed for baseball. The ball
is hiked from center field
but the backup quarterback puts it
down on a clay lump where
second base should be. The weight
of the football balanced on
a lump, awaiting a foot to kick us all
into overtime.

The Bad Girl Bicycle Poem

I wish for each poem to be a bicycle you can get
on and get off at the same time you are riding. Do not think
that the bicycle is moving, because for as long as you pedal
frequency inhibits progress toward the un-riding of the bicycle.

And so she talked on and off of bicyclical progress in
    engineering
fantasy and spirituality around which the rubber bladders
    revolve. Spoke
plainly on chained material gearing up for changing course
    before a break.
I try finding words linking Friend pulling partly hard half
    upon her seat.

Handlebars like wobbling sprockets, she's gone leaning to
    one side
and laughing mad before tightening up and leaning into the
    downhill. She's
thrilled me, caught me not looking, rode straight into me,
    and rolled
me into a ditch. Laughing, I can't help imagining how lucky
    I've been.

When in Rome

I woke up on a flimsy bed and looked
right down at the wooden floor. The room
looked nothing like my apartment, which
was where I thought I had landed the night
before. A pickaxe, a small barrel of nails
with a hammer resting on top of it was across
from me. A roll of canvas, a stack of pulled-up
planks were leaning up against the wall where
the iron bed was. I looked at the black and gray
striped blanket atop the mattress, the filthy red
union suit I wore, a dusty mirror hung next to an
oil-papered window. I found clothes, a worn-out
pair of dungarees and a green gingham shirt. I dressed
and pulled on the only pair of brogans in the room.
No sense in wasting time, I said. I looked into
the mirror and greased my hair down. *Today is the big day.*
I pulled the knuckleduster from my pocket and knew
what I had to do.

The Screw

Close to the door where I scanned
in my ID card every day a screw
was twisted into the carpet. I walked
by it all the time. One day, when nobody
was looking, I unfolded my pocketknife
and unscrewed it. I pulled up the unglued
portion of the carpet and found a bolted door.
It led to somewhere. I saw a tiny flight of steps
leading down to some kind of storage
area. I wedged down the steps, closed
the door, and made my way out of there.
The darkness was horrible. I couldn't see my
hands, although I felt one or two things
crawling underneath me. I heard clicking
ahead of me. The tunnel was too tight for
me to turn back, and so I squeezed
through without stopping toward the sound.
I felt sweat roll down my face. I panicked,
hit a wall and blacked out. When I awoke,
I still stood. I felt a doorknob in front
of me. I twisted and pushed, and here I am now,
looking at a gold watch everyone chipped in
to give me.

The Full Record

We can call gravy whatever we want.
Elizabeth Evans

The memorial crew had run into
a dry season of picking out points
of interest. The residence and final
resting place of Andrew Jackson.
The lunch counter in Greensboro where
blacks civilly disobeyed laws against
their eating lunch in white places.
Battles of Manassas and Chancellorsville.
Sieges at Yorktown and parts surrounding.
More palaces of fallen presidents
and celebratory writers, last stands, first
homes, even the roads and trails
between all the forts, theaters,
peach orchards, wheat and cornfields
had marks, monuments, scatterings
of medals and blossoming statuaries.
There came a moment when the monument
crews stood workless in the thankless
job of remembering what had happened.
It was as if collective memory stopped, and

we went on continuing the markless present
that in itself was worthless. Beyond births
and deaths of people whom history didn't
care a damn about, no moment could be found to remember
any more than previously benighted. *Peace on
Earth,* the chairman said. *Let's party!*